awake

RISE TO YOUR DIVINE ASSIGNMENT

STUDY GUIDE

www.ingramcontent.com/pod-product-compliance
Lightning Source LLC
LaVergne TN
LVHW052038080426
835513LV00018B/2378

awake

RISE TO YOUR DIVINE ASSIGNMENT

STUDY GUIDE

SARAH WEHRLI

STUDY GUIDE

awake

RISE TO YOUR DIVINE ASSIGNMENT

SARAH WEHRLI

contents

awake

A Note from Sarah:

I am so thrilled that you have joined me for this *Awake* Bible study!
This study guide is written in such a way that it can be done on
your own or within a small group. In each section, there is space for
reflection to journal what you are learning in each chapter as well as
what steps you are going to take in applying what God is speaking to
you about. This section can also be used as a starting point for small
group discussion if you desire to do this study within a group. I pray
as you read, study, and meditate on these truths that they would
come alive to you and encourage you in your unique purpose!

With Love,

Sarah

awake

Each of us is valuable to God and to the Body of Christ. Are you fully awake to that role? Have you been awakened to your assignment?

Reading Time

As you read Chapter 1: "Awake" in *Awake*, reflect on the questions and scriptures.

Reflect and Take Action:

As we begin to wake up to God's purpose for our lives, we will quickly find that His purposes are "others-centered." In other words, they revolve around people. As we fulfill God's plan for our lives, we will draw others closer to Him.

What are one or two areas in which God is calling you to "awaken"?

_____

_____

_____

_____

_____

_____

_____

Do you have a hard time believing in your value and worth to God and His mission? Why or why not?

_____

_____

_____

_____

_____

_____

_____

_____

Reflect on

Romans 13:11-14 (MSG)

But make sure that you don't get so absorbed and exhausted in taking care of all your day-by-day obligations that you lose track of the time and doze off, oblivious to God. The night is about over, dawn is about to break. Be up and awake to what God is doing! God is putting the finishing touches on the salvation work he began when we first believed. We can't afford to waste a minute, must not squander these precious daylight hours in frivolity and indulgence, in sleeping around and dissipation, in bickering and grabbing everything in sight. Get out of bed and get dressed! Don't loiter and linger, waiting until the very last minute. Dress yourselves in Christ and be up and about!

What challenges or obstacles are currently hindering you from fully awakening to your purpose?

_____

_____

_____

_____

_____

_____

How does Jesus' example in Mark 6:34 show us the importance of pressing on in our purpose—even in the midst of pain and grief?

_____

_____

_____

_____

_____

How have you already seen God use you to fulfill His purposes and draw others to Him?

_____

_____

_____

_____

_____

_____

_____

On the other hand, whom has God used to draw YOU closer to Him? Whose lives have been instrumental in your relationship with Christ?

_____

_____

_____

_____

_____

_____

_____

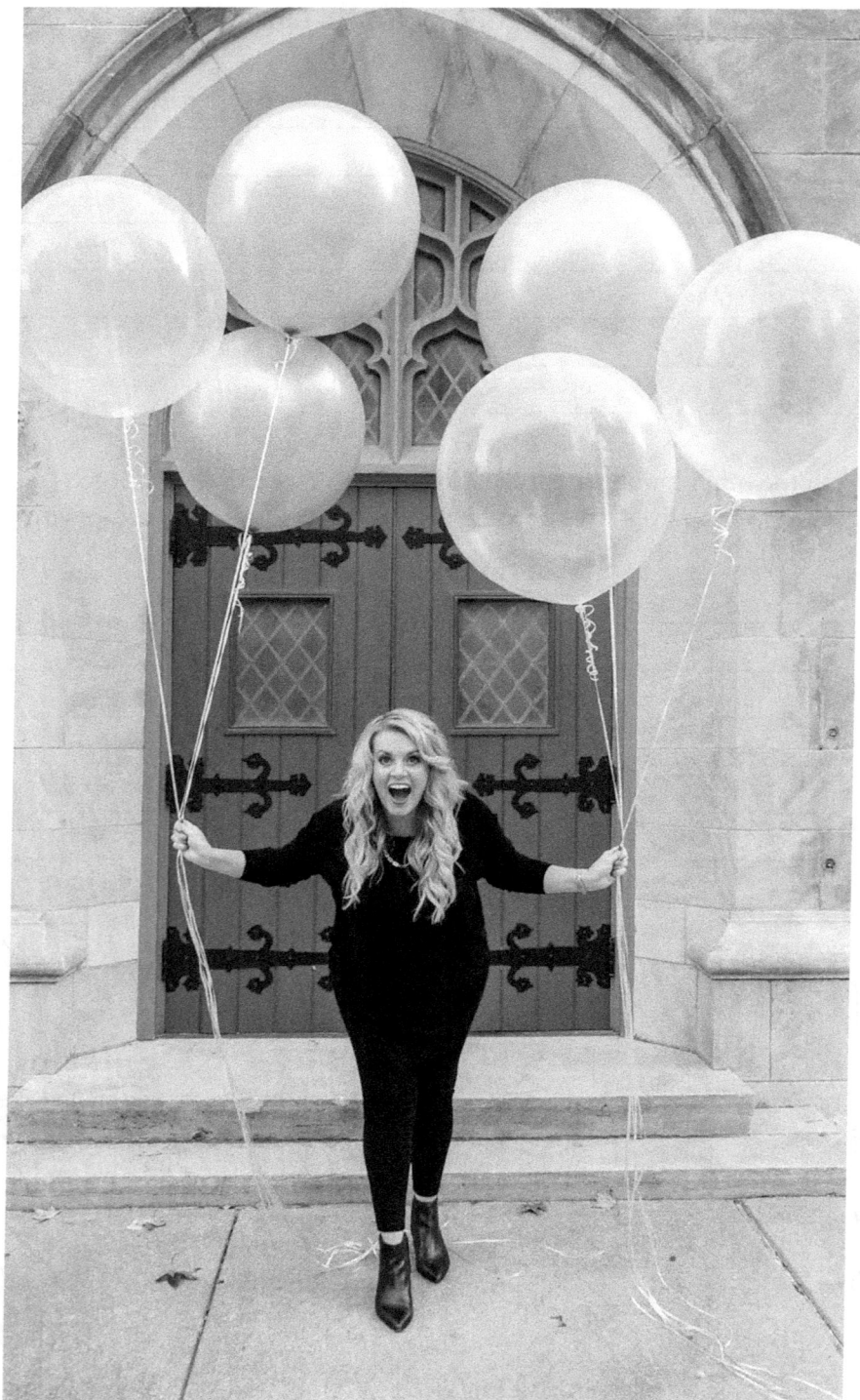

What does the following statement mean to you? "There are always people on the other side of our obedience."

_____

_____

_____

_____

_____

_____

Take time to pray and ask God to reveal His truth to you in this area—to help you awaken to the purposes and plans He has for you and overcome anything that might stand in the way of those plans!

_____

_____

_____

_____

_____

_____

What are you expecting God to do in your life in this season and through this study?

_____

_____

_____

_____

_____

_____

_____

rise up

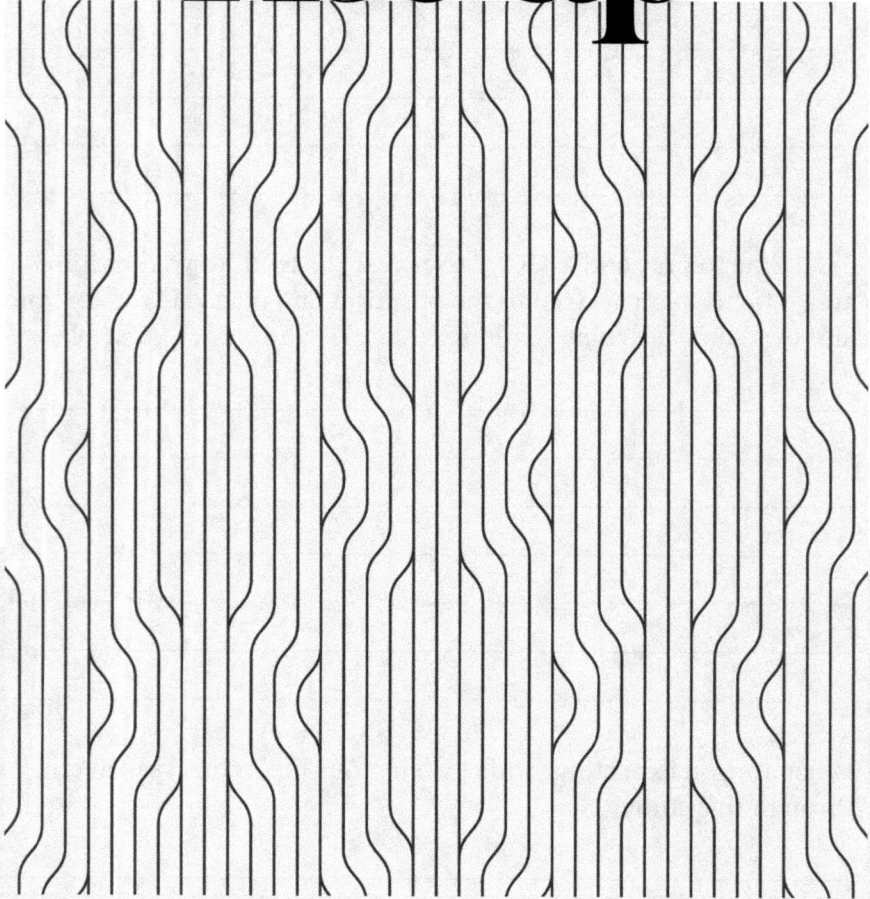

When we RISE UP and begin to understand who we are in Christ, we start to see our lives from a much different perspective.

Reading Time

As you read Chapter 2: "Rise Up" in *Awake*, reflect on the questions and scriptures.

Reflect and Take Action:

Arise means to get up—as from a sitting position—to awaken, to move upward. You may be in a place where you feel beaten down by circumstances and depression, but God is calling you to rise to a new life. He has a beautiful purpose for your life.

God's Word has creative power. Take a look back at these verses, write them out, and begin to speak them over your life. Here is what God says about you and your future:

Jeremiah 29:11-13

_____

_____

_____

_____

_____

_____

_____

_____

_____

_____

Ephesians 2:10

_____

_____

_____

_____

_____

"Arise [from spiritual depression to a new life], shine [be radiant with the glory and brilliance of the LORD]; for your light has come, And the glory and brilliance of the LORD has risen upon you. "For in fact, darkness will cover the earth And deep darkness will cover the peoples; But the LORD will rise upon you [Jerusalem] And His glory and brilliance will be seen on you. Nations will come to your light, And kings to the brightness of your rising."

Psalm 139:13-18

_____

_____

_____

_____

_____

_____

1 Peter 2:9

_____

_____

_____

_____

_____

_____

_____

1 Corinthians 2:9-10

_____

_____

_____

_____

_____

_____

_____

Why is it important that we "give out" of ourselves on a regular basis? What are some ways you are "giving out" to others?

_____

_____

_____

_____

_____

_____

_____

Do you struggle with comparison? If so, how? What tends to make you feel insecure when you begin to compare yourself with others?

_____

_____

_____

_____

_____

_____

_____

How does Psalm 139:14-15 reinforce the value and uniqueness of your calling? After reading this passage, what new thoughts or feelings do you have regarding God's one-of-a-kind call on you to rise up?

_____

_____

_____

_____

_____

_____

_____

What talents and abilities can you perceive in yourself that God placed there to help others and make the world a better place?

_____

_____

_____

_____

_____

_____

What action steps do you sense God is calling you to take in light of this chapter's truths?

_____

_____

_____

_____

_____

_____

the greatest treasure

God has so much in store for us. But we must take the time to get to know Him.

Reflect and Take Action:

God is speaking vision to His Church and to us individually, but we must remain tuned in and ready to hear with ears of faith. With all the voices vying for our attention, we must be still and hear what He is saying.

What is the greatest treasure we should seek according to Matthew 6:33?

_____

_____

_____

_____

_____

_____

_____

How has God surprised you in the way He's brought His promises and blessings to pass in your life? How have His ways differed from your expectations?

_____

_____

_____

_____

_____

_____

_____

Reflect on

Jeremiah 29:12-13 (NIV)

"Then you will call on me and come and pray to me, and I will listen to you. You will seek me and find me when you seek me with all your heart."

How has knowing God more fully led you to discover the incredible treasures of His Word?

_____

_____

_____

_____

_____

_____

_____

_____

What are some of the ways God speaks to us and directs us according to John 1:1, Psalm 119:105, and John 10:27?

_____

_____

_____

_____

_____

_____

_____

_____

How are you making daily time to listen to and heed God's voice? Where would you like to grow in this area?

_____

_____

_____

_____

_____

_____

_____

What are places, times, or environments in which you find that you're most able to hear God's voice?

_____

_____

_____

_____

_____

_____

_____

How has God's Word kept you on track to reach your destination? How has it helped you avoid detours or getting lost?

_____

_____

_____

_____

_____

_____

_____

Conversely, when have you ever gotten off track during a season in which you weren't regularly in God's Word?

_____

_____

_____

_____

_____

_____

_____

_____

_____

Sarah writes, "God has a purpose for every single day, and He says if we will put Him first in each one, He will direct our path." What potential purposes do you see for today? How can you surrender yourself to God so that He can fulfill those purposes?

_____

_____

_____

_____

_____

_____

_____

_____

_____

armed and dangerous

We put on our strength daily as we spend time meditating on God's Word, speaking it boldly, and lifting our praise and worship to Him.

Reading Time

As you read Chapter 4: "Armed and Dangerous" in *Awake*, reflect on the questions and scriptures.

Reflect and Take Action:

When we speak His Word in the midst of problems, we are taking up our sword and using our authority as a believer.

Why is it so essential to seek God for strength every single day?

_____

_____

_____

_____

_____

_____

_____

_____

_____

What are the things you're praying for and believing God for currently?

_____

_____

_____

_____

_____

_____

_____

_____

_____

Reflect on

Ephesians 6:10-18 (NIV)

Be strong in the Lord and in His mighty power. Put on the full armor of God, so that you can take your stand against the devil's schemes. For our struggle is not against flesh and blood, but against the rulers ... of this dark world and against the spiritual forces of evil in the heavenly realms. Therefore put on the full armor of God, so that when the day of evil comes, you may be able to stand your ground, and after you have done everything, to stand. Stand firm then, with the belt of truth buckled around your waist, with the breastplate of righteousness in place, and with your feet fitted with the readiness that comes from the gospel of peace. In addition to all this, take up the shield of faith, with which you can extinguish all the flaming arrows of the evil one. Take the helmet of salvation and the sword of the Spirit, which is the word of God. And pray in the Spirit on all occasions with all kinds of prayers and requests.

How can you "feed your faith" regarding these specific things you are praying for?

_____

_____

_____

_____

_____

_____

_____

_____

_____

_____

_____

_____

What are some specific scriptures you are standing on regarding those things?

_____

_____

_____

_____

_____

_____

_____

Who are two or three people of faith who can stand with you and agree with you for what you're praying for?

_____

_____

_____

_____

_____

_____

_____

Why is it important to remember that the battle doesn't belong to us? What risks do we run by believing that we have to do everything on our own?

_____

_____

_____

_____

_____

_____

_____

shake it off

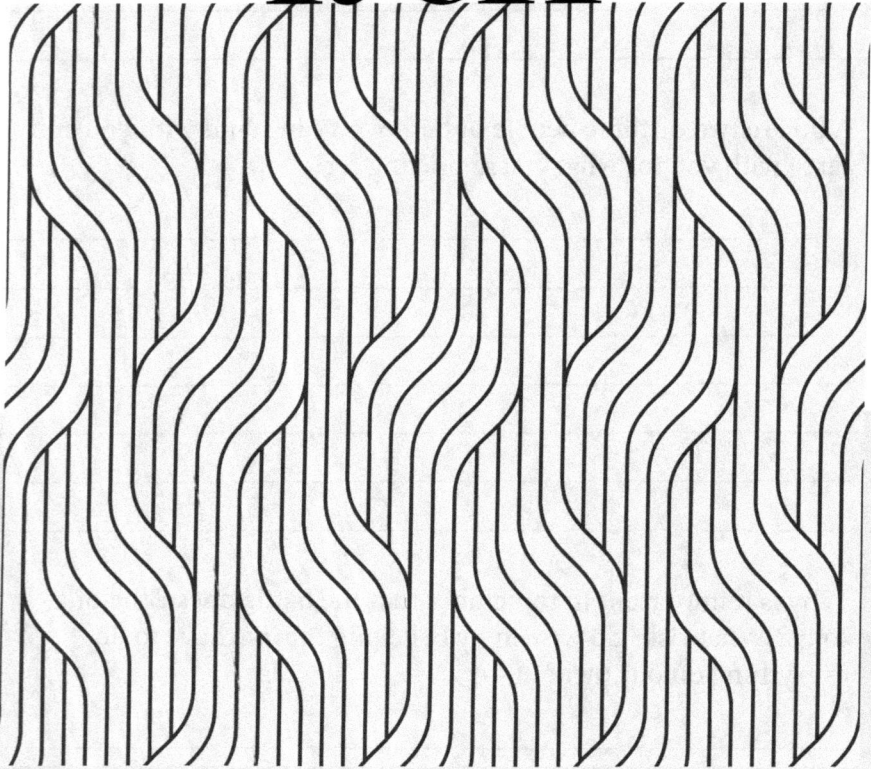

> God has a purpose for us to fulfill, so it's time to get up out of our pit, shake off the dust, and rise up as a light in this world.

Reading Time

As you read Chapter 5: "Shake It Off" in *Awake,* reflect on the questions and scriptures.

Reflect and Take Action:

When we are tempted to get caught up in comparison, we need to remember that God won't help us become anyone else except the person He created us to be.

What did Gideon have to "shake off" in order to fulfill His assignment?

_____

_____

_____

_____

_____

_____

_____

_____

How are you going to "shake off" the lies of the enemy and overcome the challenges facing you?

_____

_____

_____

_____

_____

_____

_____

_____

Reflect on

Judges 6:12-18 (NASB)

The angel of the Lord appeared to him and said to him, "The Lord is with you, O valiant warrior." Then Gideon said to him, "O my lord, if the Lord is with us, why then has all this happened to us? And where are all His miracles which our fathers told us about, saying, 'Did not the Lord bring us up from Egypt?' But now the Lord has abandoned us and given us into the hand of Midian." The Lord looked at him and said, "Go in this your strength and deliver Israel from the hand of Midian. Have I not sent you?" He said to Him, "O Lord, how shall I deliver Israel? Behold, my family is the least in Manasseh, and I am the youngest in my father's house." But the Lord said to him, "Surely I will be with you, and you shall defeat Midian as one man." So, Gideon said to Him, "If now I have found favor in Your sight, then show me a sign that it is You who speak with me. Please do not depart from here, until I come back to You, and bring out my offering and lay it before You." And He said, "I will remain until you return."

Take some time to write down some of the scriptures you are declaring over your life and circumstances.

_____

_____

_____

_____

_____

_____

_____

_____

_____

Why do you think God didn't acknowledge Gideon's protests, but instead responded that He would be with Gideon? How did this alter Gideon's perspective? How does it alter yours?

_____

_____

_____

_____

_____

_____

_____

When have you stepped out in obedience even amid feelings of fear or apprehension? What did this do to strengthen your faith in God?

_____

_____

_____

_____

_____

_____

_____

How is God calling you to step out in faith right now? What practical steps can you take to obey His leading?

_____

_____

_____

_____

_____

_____

_____

fresh and flourishing

What will help us stay fresh and flourishing every day? Keeping God's life consistently flowing through us and continually renewing our minds with His Word will keep Him near.

Reading Time

As you read Chapter 6: "Fresh and Flourishing" in *Awake*, reflect on the questions and scriptures.

Reflect and Take Action:

There is a refueling that takes place in the presence of God. Your natural ability can only take you so far, but as you wait on God and spend time in His presence, He will renew your strength and give you fresh insight in the areas you need it.

How does our spirit differ from our mind in terms of renewal? How does salvation affect both areas?

_____

_____

_____

_____

_____

_____

_____

Describe a time you felt like you were in a "tug of war" between your spirit and flesh.

_____

_____

_____

_____

_____

_____

_____

_____

_____

Reflect on

Romans 12:1-2 (MSG)

So, here's what I want you to do, God helping you: Take your everyday, ordinary life—your sleeping, eating, going-to-work, and walking-around life—and place it before God as an offering. Embracing what God does for you is the best thing you can do for him. Don't become so well-adjusted to your culture that you fit into it without even thinking. Instead, fix your attention on God. You'll be changed from the inside out. Readily recognize what he wants from you, and quickly respond to it. Unlike the culture around you, always dragging you down to its level of immaturity, God brings the best out of you, develops well-formed maturity in you.

What can you do to "strengthen your spirit"?

_____

_____

_____

_____

_____

_____

_____

_____

_____

_____

_____

_____

How do we produce "good fruit" according to Psalm 1:1-3?

_____

_____

_____

_____

_____

_____

_____

_____

_____

_____

Why is it impossible to produce anything of lasting value without being connected to Jesus and His Word daily? When have you tried to do this apart from Him? What did you learn from that experience?

_____

_____

_____

_____

_____

_____

_____

_____

_____

_____

_____

_____

Explain this truth in your own words: "God has called us to be rivers of His love, not reservoirs."

_____

_____

_____

_____

_____

_____

_____

_____

_____

_____

Who can you reach out to today who needs God's love? How can you practically be the hands and feet of Jesus to this person?

_____

_____

_____

_____

_____

_____

_____

_____

_____

_____

_____

a life of love

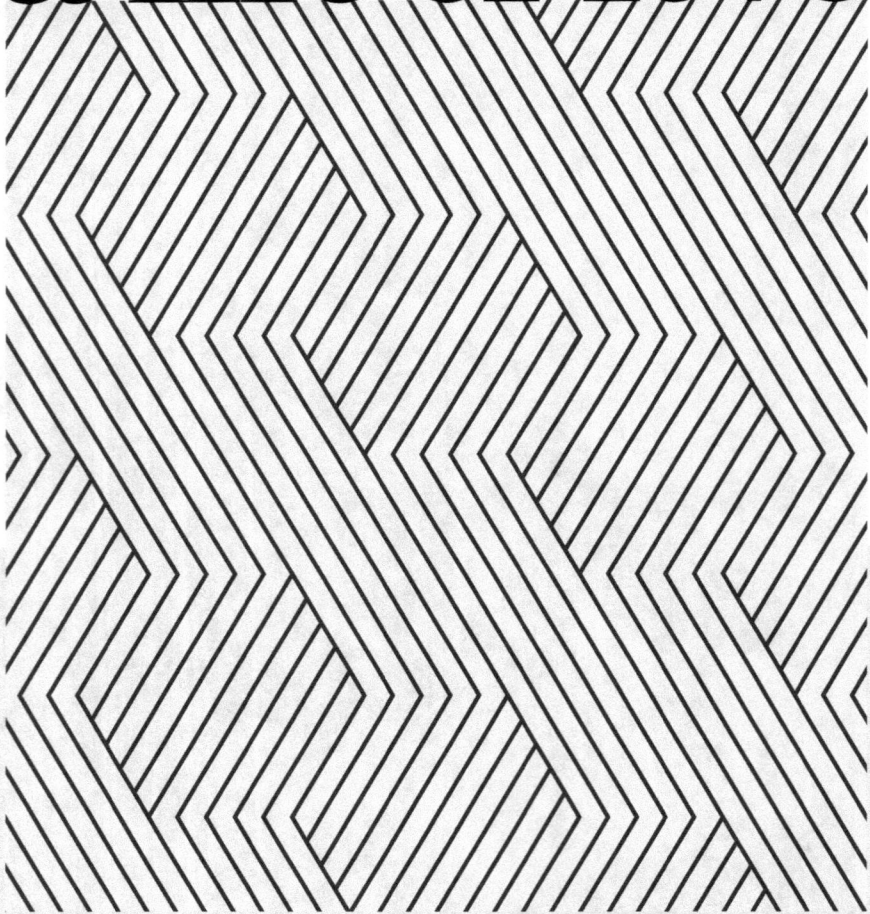

We, as children of God, are called to imitate Him in the world we live in. We are called to have His kind of love that reaches out to the hurting, hopeless, and broken.

Reading Time

As you read Chapter 7: "A Life of Love" in *Awake*, reflect on the questions and scriptures.

Reflect and Take Action:

Be sensitive and let Him interrupt you so you can share His love with those you come into contact with. It's amazing how quickly joy comes when we get our eyes off ourselves and begin to help someone else.

Who may be waiting on the other side of your obedience?

_____

_____

_____

_____

_____

_____

_____

_____

How can we live a life of love toward those close to us as well as those we come into contact with?

_____

_____

_____

_____

_____

_____

_____

Reflect on

Mark 4:35-41; 5:1-2 (ESV)

On that day, when evening had come, he said to them, "Let us go across to the other side." And leaving the crowd, they took him with them in the boat, just as he was. And other boats were with him. And a great windstorm arose, and the waves were breaking into the boat, so that the boat was already filling. But he was in the stern, asleep on the cushion. And they woke him and said to him, "Teacher, do you not care that we are perishing?" And he awoke and rebuked the wind and said to the sea, "Peace! Be still!" And the wind ceased, and there was a great calm. He said to them, "Why are you so afraid? Have you still no faith?" And they were filled with great fear and said to one another, "Who then is this, that even the wind and the sea obey him?"

They came to the other side of the sea, to the country of the Gerasenes. And when Jesus had stepped out of the boat, immediately there met him out of the tombs a man with an unclean spirit.

What does it mean to live with "eternity in mind"?

_____

_____

_____

_____

_____

_____

_____

_____

_____

_____

What does this statement mean to you? "One moment of your time could mean eternity to someone else."

_____

_____

_____

_____

_____

_____

Are there people God has put in your sphere of influence who don't know Him? Is there a people group God has put on your heart to witness to? If so, make a list of their names to begin praying for them.

_____

_____

_____

_____

_____

_____

Do you think believers today have a proper sense of urgency about sharing the gospel with those who don't know Christ? Explain your answer.

_____

_____

_____

_____

_____

_____

How does serving others equate to serving Jesus according to this chapter?

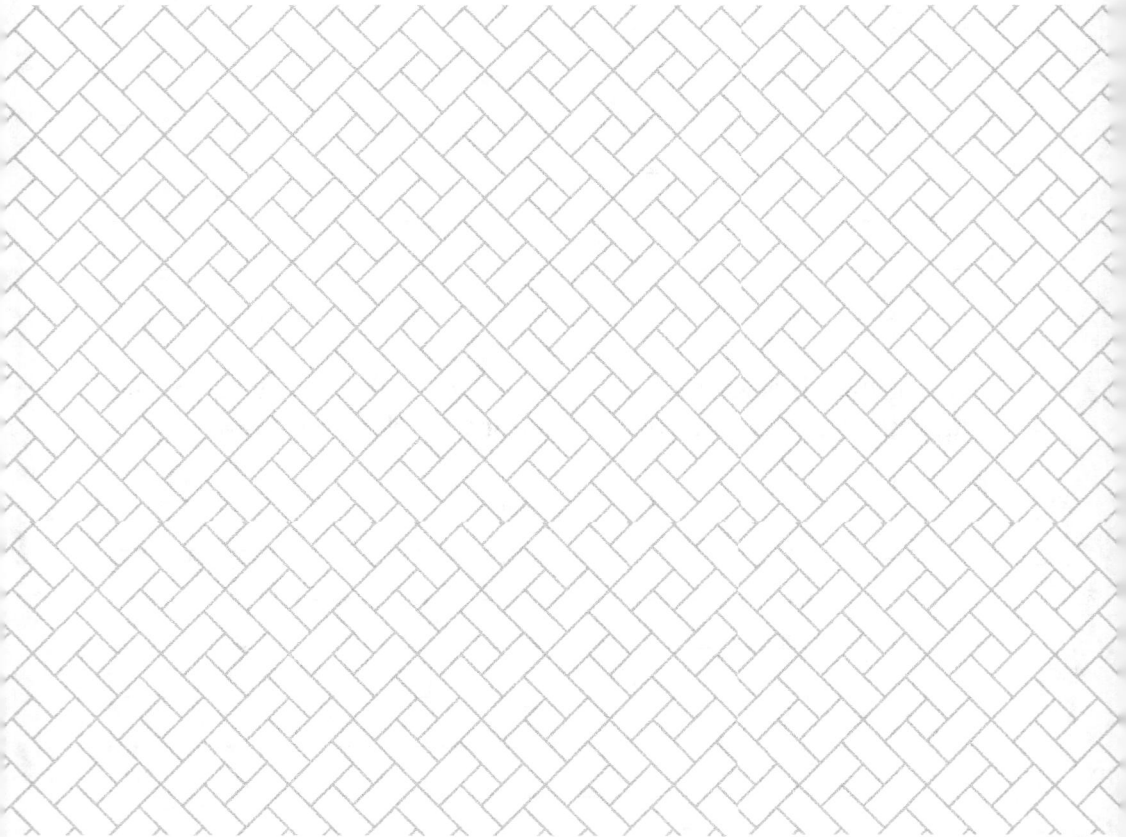

_____

_____

_____

_____

_____

_____

_____

_____

_____

Write down what God has been speaking to you and the steps you are going to take to obey His voice.

_____

_____

_____

_____

_____

_____

_____

_____

_____

what's in your hand?

He has given each of us gifts, talents, opportunities, influence, and resources, but they don't do us any good unless we recognize the purpose for them and the power that's available to us in Christ.

Reading Time

As you read
Chapter 8:
"What's in
Your Hand?" in
Awake, reflect
on the questions
and scriptures.

Reflect and Take Action:

God has put things in your hands to bring Him glory and make a difference in the lives of others for His kingdom.

What has God put in your hand? Take some time to write down the talents, strengths, opportunities, influence, and resources that God has given you.

_____

_____

_____

_____

_____

_____

_____

How might these be used to benefit others and show them the truth and love of Christ?

_____

_____

_____

_____

_____

_____

_____

_____

_____

_____

Reflect on

Exodus 4:1-17 (NIV)

Moses answered, "What if they do not believe me or listen to me and say, 'The LORD did not appear to you'?"

Then the LORD said to him, "What is that in your hand?"

"A staff," he replied.

The LORD said, "Throw it on the ground."

Moses threw it on the ground, and it became a snake, and he ran from it. Then the LORD said to him, "Reach out your hand and take it by the tail." So Moses reached out and took hold of the snake and it turned back into a staff in his hand. "This," said the LORD, "is so that they may believe that the LORD, the God of their fathers—the God of Abraham, the God of Isaac and the God of Jacob—has appeared to you."

Then the LORD said, "Put your hand inside your cloak." So Moses put his hand into his cloak, and when he took it out, the skin was leprous—it had become as white as snow.

"Now put it back into your cloak," he said. So, Moses put his hand back into his cloak, and when he took it out, it was restored, like the rest of his flesh.

How have you already seen God use your talents and influence to benefit others?

_____

_____

_____

_____

_____

_____

_____

> Then the LORD said, "If they do not believe you or pay attention to the first sign, they may believe the second. But if they do not believe these two signs or listen to you, take some water from the Nile and pour it on the dry ground. The water you take from the river will become blood on the ground."
>
> Moses said to the LORD, "Pardon your servant, Lord. I have never been eloquent, neither in the past nor since you have spoken to your servant. I am slow of speech and tongue."
>
> The LORD said to him, "Who gave human beings their mouths? Who makes them deaf or mute? Who gives them sight or makes them blind? Is it not I, the LORD? Now go; I will help you speak and will teach you what to say."
>
> But Moses said, "Pardon your servant, Lord. Please send someone else."
>
> Then the LORD's anger burned against Moses and he said, "What about your brother, Aaron the Levite? I know he can speak well. He is already on his way to meet you, and he will be glad to see you. You shall speak to him and put words in his mouth; I will help both of you speak and will teach you what to do. He will speak to the people for you, and it will be as if he were your mouth and as if you were God to him. But take this staff in your hand so you can perform the signs with it."

Conversely, how have others' gifts and resources benefitted you?

_____

_____

_____

_____

_____

_____

_____

What you have right now may not seem like much, but God can still use it! Which story in this chapter showed you this truth most effectively?

_____

_____

_____

_____

_____

_____

What are some ways you can begin to use what God has put in your hand? Write down some steps you can take this week and in the coming months.

_____

_____

_____

_____

_____

_____

_____

_____

_____

_____

_____

_____

_____

_____

being stretched

*God's vision for your life will cause you to expand.
It will cause you to stretch—you will give more than
you have ever given, love more than you have ever
loved, and believe more than you have ever believed.*

Reading Time

As you read Chapter 9: "Being Stretched" in *Awake*, reflect on the questions and scriptures.

Reflect and Take Action:

In order to enlarge, expand, and reach more people for Christ, we must step out in faith to do what God is asking us to do, regardless of whether it requires us to do something new or go somewhere unfamiliar.

What has God been speaking to you about that seems too big for you to handle?

_____

_____

_____

_____

_____

_____

_____

_____

How does this calling make you uncomfortable or lead you into unfamiliar territory?

_____

_____

_____

_____

_____

_____

_____

_____

Reflect on

Isaiah 54:2-3 (NKJV)

"Enlarge the place of your tent,

And let them stretch out the curtains of your dwellings;

Do not spare;

Lengthen your cords

And strengthen your stakes.

For you shall expand to the right and to the left,

And your descendants will inherit the nations,

And make the desolate cities inhabited."

What will it cost you to "launch out" in obedience to God's calling in this area? What will you gain?

_____

_____

_____

_____

_____

_____

_____

_____

_____

_____

_____

_____

Why do you think Jesus often asked His followers to do things that didn't make sense in the natural?

_____

_____

_____

_____

_____

_____

What are some steps you can take today and this month to lead you into those dreams God has put in your heart?

_____

_____

_____

_____

_____

_____

_____

Whom will your obedience benefit? Who will be changed as a result of your stepping out and being stretched?

_____

_____

_____

_____

_____

_____

travel light

*When we spend time in God's presence and His Word,
He begins to reveal to us things we need to let go of.*

Reading
Time

As you read
Chapter 10:
"Travel Light"
in *Awake*, reflect
on the questions
and scriptures.

Reflect and Take Action:

*Many times, we try to hang on to the old
things—old habits and mindsets—but those
things will only slow us down when we go
where God wants to take us.*

How can you "make room" for the new
things God desires to bring in your life?

_____

_____

_____

_____

_____

_____

_____

_____

What is hindering you or slowing you down
from going forward in the plan God has for
you?

_____

_____

_____

_____

_____

_____

_____

_____

Reflect on

Isaiah 43:18-19 (NKJV)

"Do not remember the former things,

Nor consider the things of old.

Behold, I will do a new thing,

Now it shall spring forth ...

I will even make a road in the wilderness

And rivers in the desert."

Hebrews 12:1-2 (NIV)

Therefore, since we are surrounded by such a great cloud of witnesses, let us throw off everything that hinders and the sin that so easily entangles. And let us run with perseverance the race marked out for us, fixing our eyes on Jesus, the pioneer and perfecter of faith. For the joy set before him he endured the cross, scorning its shame, and sat down at the right hand of the throne of God.

What "limiting" thoughts are "fencing you in"? How can you let them go?

_____

_____

_____

_____

_____

_____

_____

_____

Think about a person in the Bible whom you admire who rose to the assignment God had for them. How does their story relate to yours? What have you learned from their story?

_____

_____

_____

_____

_____

_____

_____

_____

_____

_____

What action steps is God leading you to take in light of this chapter? Spend some time praying about them and surrendering to God in these areas.

_____

_____

_____

_____

_____

_____

_____

_____

_____

_____

joy on the journey

Joy is not based on our circumstances; it's based on our hope and faith in Jesus Christ.

Reading Time

As you read Chapter 11: "Joy on the Journey" in *Awake*, reflect on the questions and scriptures.

Reflect and Take Action:

When we choose to walk in joy during our journey, we will be sensitive to those around us who need hope and healing. We will be sensitive to those who need to know that Jesus is the only way, truth, and life.

What are some areas you need to trust God in concerning your life and future?

_____

_____

_____

_____

_____

_____

According to Nehemiah 8:10, why is it so important that we rejoice and choose joy?

_____

_____

_____

_____

_____

_____

_____

Reflect on

Philippians 4:4-9 (ESV)

Rejoice in the Lord always; again, I will say, rejoice. Let your reasonableness be known to everyone. The Lord is at hand; do not be anxious about anything, but in everything by prayer and supplication with thanksgiving let your requests be made known to God. And the peace of God, which surpasses all understanding, will guard your hearts and your minds in Christ Jesus.

Finally, brothers, whatever is true, whatever is honorable, whatever is just, whatever is pure, whatever is lovely, whatever is commendable, if there is any excellence, if there is anything worthy of praise, think about these things. What you have learned and received and heard and seen in me—practice these things, and the God of peace will be with you.

Romans 15:13 (NLT)

I pray that God, the source of hope, will fill you completely with joy and peace because you trust in him. Then you will overflow with confident hope through the power of the Holy Spirit.

Where do we find joy according to the verses above?

_____

_____

_____

_____

_____

_____

_____

One of the things Sarah says in this chapter is that "our joy is not based on hype but on our hope in Jesus." What does that mean to you? When have you found joy in the midst of challenging times because of your hope in Jesus?

_____

_____

_____

_____

_____

_____

_____

_____

_____

One of the keys to joy that Sarah shares is forgiveness. Is there anyone that you need to forgive? Take some time to pray and release that person to the Lord. Forgive them, pray God's blessings over them, and trust God to vindicate you. Let go of any hindrance that is keeping you from enjoying the journey God has for you!

_____

_____

_____

_____

_____

_____

_____

_____

_____

_____

What does it mean in Colossians 3:15 (AMP) when it says, "Let God's peace act as the 'umpire' of your heart"?

_____

_____

_____

_____

_____

_____

What can you do to cultivate your JOY?

_____

_____

_____

_____

_____

_____

How have others been a good example to you in this area? Whom do you consider your "joy role models" to be?

_____

_____

_____

_____

_____

_____

What action steps is God calling you to take in light of this chapter? What routines or practices could you set up in order to walk more fully in joy and forgiveness?

_____

_____

_____

_____

_____

_____

_____

_____

_____

_____

press on

Our life is much like the process of a seed being planted. You may not see overnight results, but if you stay faithful, consistent, and patient, the results will soon be manifest.

Reading Time

As you read Chapter 12: "Press On" in *Awake*, reflect on the questions and scriptures.

Reflect and Take Action:

Don't let the enemy distract you from your purpose. We need you to stay at your post. We need every part of the body of Christ to do their part in reaching the harvest.

What has God "assigned" you to do at this time?

_____
_____
_____
_____
_____
_____
_____
_____
_____

What are some of the dreams in your heart for the future?

_____
_____
_____
_____
_____
_____
_____
_____
_____
_____

What keys can we learn from the example of Nehemiah in fulfilling our assignment?

_____

_____

_____

_____

_____

_____

_____

_____

_____

Write down the steps you are going to take in fulfilling your unique God-given assignment. Many times, the secret to succeeding in an area is found in our daily routine, so start by writing little steps can you take toward the dreams and purpose God has put in your heart. Even if it is just a few moments a day doing something toward your dream, it makes a difference!

Take some time to write down the practical steps you are going to take in walking out your assignment in the coming days, weeks, months, and year.

Daily steps:

_____

_____

_____

_____

_____

_____

_____

_____

_____

Weekly steps:

_____

_____

_____

_____

_____

_____

_____

_____

_____

This month:

_____
_____
_____
_____
_____
_____
_____
_____
_____

This year:

_____
_____
_____
_____
_____
_____
_____
_____
_____

What is the "Ultimate Goal" according to 2 Corinthians 5:9?

_____
_____
_____
_____
_____
_____

Take some time to write down what God has spoken to you throughout this book and the lessons that have resonated with you.

_____

_____

_____

_____

_____

_____

_____

_____

_____

_____

_____

_____

_____

_____

_____

_____

_____

_____

_____

_____

_____

_____

_____

_____

_____

_____

_____

_____

_____

_____

awake

A Final Note from Sarah:

As we come to the end of this book, I want to congratulate you for completing this study and taking the time to invest in your future. I believe the time you have spent reading and meditating on God's Word will produce great fruit in your life. Be encouraged that this is only the beginning! With God, there are always new things He desires to do in and through you. His Word says He takes us from faith to faith, strength to strength, and glory to glory. The call of God is always upward!

I would LOVE to hear testimonies of what God has done in your life through this *Awake* Bible study and how it has impacted you. Feel free to email me at info@inspireintl.com and share this study with friends. It has been an honor to encourage you in your journey, and I pray for God's strength in you as you pursue the purpose He has for your life!

Cheering you on,

Sarah Wehrli